How Things Are Made

Apples to Applesauce

By Inez Snyder

Welcome
Books™

Children's Press®
A Division of Scholastic Inc.
New York / Toronto / London / Auckland / Sydney
Mexico City / New Delhi / Hong Kong
Danbury, Connecticut

Photo Credits: All photos by Maura B. McConnell

Contributing Editor: Shira Laskin
Book Design: Christopher Logan

Library of Congress Cataloging-in-Publication Data

Snyder, Inez.
   Apples to applesauce / by Inez Snyder.
   p. cm.—(How things are made)
   Includes index.
   ISBN 0-516-25195-3 (lib. bdg.)—ISBN 0-516-25525-8 (pbk.)
   1. Cookery (Apples)—Juvenile literature. 2. Applesauce—Juvenile literature. I. Title.
   II. Series.

   TX813.A6S64 2005
   641.6'411—dc22

                                            2004010333

Contents

Applesauce is made from apples.

First, the apples are **peeled**.

The skin is taken off each apple.

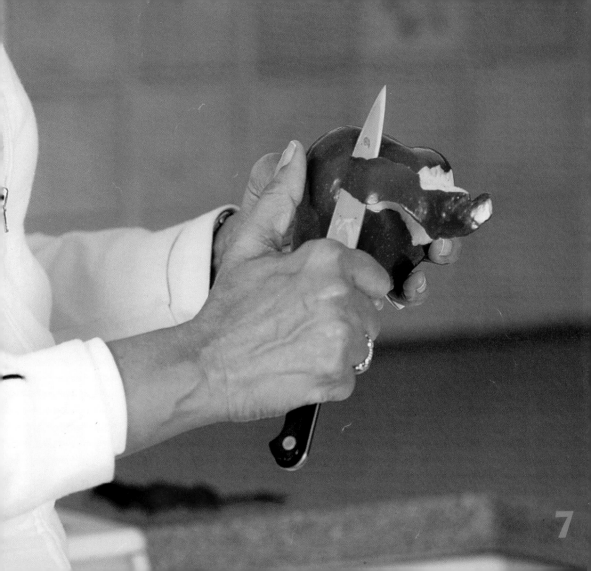

Then, the apples are cut into small pieces.

The pieces of apple are put into a pot with water.

Sugar and **cinnamon** are also put into the pot.

They will make the apples taste **sweet**.

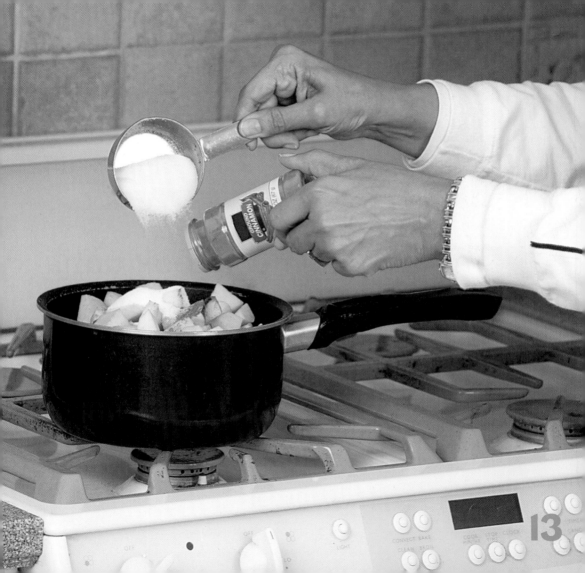

The apples must cook until they are soft.

Once the apples are soft, they can be **mashed**.

Now, they are applesauce.

The applesauce is put into **jars**.

The applesauce is ready to be eaten.

It is fun to make applesauce!

New Words

applesauce (**ap**-uhl-sawss) a food made from apples that are cooked until soft with spices and water

cinnamon (**sin**-uh-muhn) a spice that comes from the bark of a tropical tree

jars (**jahrz**) short, wide bottles that are often made of glass and have covers that can be put on and taken off

mashed (**mashd**) crushed into a smooth mixture

peeled (**peeld**) to have taken the skin or outside layer of something off

sugar (**shug**-ur) a white or brown food that comes from a plant and is used to make other foods sweet

sweet (**sweet**) having the taste of sugar or honey

To Find Out More

Books
Apple
by Angela Royston
Heinemann Library

Applesauce
by Shirley Kurtz
Good Books

Web Sites
PBS Kids: Mister Rogers's Neighborhood Applesauce Recipe
http://pbskids.org/rogers/R_house/recipe5.htm
Follow this recipe with an adult to make your
own applesauce.

U.S. Apple Association Kids' Page
http://www.usapple.org/consumers/kids/index.shtml
Learn about apples and print out pictures to color from
this Web site.

Index

About the Author
Inez Snyder writes books to help children learn how to read.

Content Consultant
Jason Farrey, The Culinary Institute

Reading Consultants
Kris Flynn, Coordinator, Small School District Literacy, The San Diego County Office of Education

Shelly Forys, Certified Reading Recovery Specialist, W.J. Zahnow Elementary School, Waterloo, IL

Paulette Mansell, Certified Reading Recovery Specialist, and Early Literacy Consultant, TX